Introduction

This is a book of tips that you can easily deploy, driving more traffic to your website. This is the second edition with updated tips for 52 weeks – so just do one thing each week. We have also now added and updated a few longer articles from our online publishing activities to give you much more in depth strategies for marketing online.

You may be wondering why this is not a big book of detailed actions or set by step processes? I wanted provide some useful, easy to digest and, more importantly, easy to implement ideas.

As a busy broker, you don't have the time to read pages and pages of stuff. A 200 page book is likely to dishearten you to inaction, so I hope by taking an easier approach, you will implement a few of these techniques.

Not all of them will be applicable to you but there will be enough here that if you deploy even 10% of them, they will drive more traffic and enquires to your website.

Don't feel you have to follow each one. Scan through them and highlight the ones that appeal to you, and get implementing.

Good Luck!

Jason Hulott

Director
Speedie Consulting
http://www.speedieconsulting.co.uk

Insurance Marketing Tips

1. **Title Tags**

   Title Tags appear in the header of your browser when visiting a webpage. They are also used by search engines when displaying results.

   Insert your major keywords into the title tags of your pages. Make sure that the keywords you use appear on the content of the site. For example Use "cheap car insurance" if the phrase appears on the page. The more important the keyword, the nearer the beginning of the title it should be.

   Do not use the same title for every page on your site – doing this will see your site penalised. Make sure each page has its own unique title.

2. **Link Titles**

   Link titles help define a link and also can show up when a user moves over them within their browser using a mouse.

   To give your links more value and to make then useable by various browsers, you can add a title in the code of the link.

   For Example

   ```
   <a href=http://www.mywebsite.com"
   title="Compare Car Insurance">
   ```

3. **Find the best Keywords**

    Use the Keyword Tool website to find high traffic, highly searched keyword phrases for your business, then spend some time research and drilling down into different lists and combinations of words. There will be some hidden goldmines in there.

    Keyword Tools will then give you a range of topics that you can write about and some text for linking structures between internal pages on your website.

    Visit www.keywordtool.io

4. **Image Alt Texts**

    Image Alt Text allows you to label an image so it has a description. This has been used in the past to try and stuff keywords, but used correctly it can help identify images and rank them.

Make sure you are using descriptive keyword based alt text to your images. The image alt text will appear if the image doesn't load and gives a descriptive phrase to help explain what the images is about.

For Example

< img src="http://www.mywebsite.com/images/mymage1.gif" alt="This is my descriptive text">

If you are not using alt text then make sure you do this as a matter of some importance. Alt tags can boost your site's ability to rank for its keywords. It also makes the site more user friendly.

5.   **Add multiple Sitemaps**

Sitemaps are now a standard way to notify Search engines of all your site pages. Using a sitemap is also useful for visitors who may get lost searching your site. Add a HTML site map for those visitors. Build and add an XML version for Google and a Text version for Yahoo.

Use Sitemapbuilder.net and download the free tool. With this you can build all your sitemaps.

To upload the XML site map to Google you will need to register with Google Webmaster Tools

http://www.google.com/webmasters

For Bing you need to register with Bing Webmaster Tools

To make sure it gets picked up by all search engines get your web guy to add it to your robots.txt file (Don't worry they'll know what that is).

6.   **Robots.txt File**

Following on from the last note, a Robots.txt file is a small text file that allows you to tell a search engine spider what it can and cannot see on your website.

It means you can stop it visiting protected areas or development areas of the site you don't want visitors to see.   It also allows you to tell the spiders where your sitemap is.

You can simply build a robots.txt file using notepad.

Take care when amending or adding a robots.txt file, one false move and you can stop spiders visiting your pages.

Read this page:

7.   **Guest Posting**

Writing useful, readable articles about your products and services, and submitting them online to other related websites who may allow you to become a guest author, is a great way to attract search engines and direct traffic. Make sure the article is useful and not just a sales pitch.

There are a number of ways to find sites to submit content to.

Use Google and search for

"Guest posts + KEYWORD"

"Contributor + KEYWORD"

"Become an Author + KEYWORD"

Make sure you create a resource "About the Author" box and add links back to your company website and/or social media pages.

8. **Press Releases**

As well as writing and sending out a press release to the media, you can also add it to various Press Release websites that will list your press release for free. It can drive traffic, get your site noticed by Google and add good quality links back to your website.

Press Release Syndication Sites include:
www.prfire.co.uk
www.prlog.org

9. **Trade or Swap Articles with other sites**

As well as syndicating articles on major sites

which, we touched on above, find relevant sites in your industry or of interest to your ideal client base and trade articles. This could be one of your business partner sites such as an Accountant or other professional body. If you do this, make the article unique to them to give it some added value.

10.   **Build a News Section**

Write about, and link to, companies with "in the news" pages. They link back to stories and blog posts, which cover their developments. This is obviously easiest if you have a news section or blog. Setup Google news alerts around your major keywords and set it to once a day. Visit trade or other news services such as NewsNow.co.uk

Use these to rewrite your own little news section in your industry. Then share stories on social media. If you are using WordPress to run your site you can automate the sharing of content.

11.   **Trade Links with Professional Bodies and Partners**

Get links to your site from any trade organisation you are a member of. This could include local chamber of commerce, Professional Bodies, Network members or partners.

12.   **Use Classified Ads**

Using a Classified ad to promote a product or service or use to promote a free gift in order to build your mailing list. Write a 50 to 100 word small ad. Pay attention to the headline as this is grabber than will get people to open your ad.

Some Classified ad sites have thousands of visits a day so it is a worthwhile exercise to post an ad once a month.

Visit and post in the right categories in your local area using:

www.vivastreet.co.uk
www.gumtree.com

13. **Build Webpages outside your website**

Sites such as www.hubpages.com , www.quora.com or www.medium.com allow users to build pages on topics of their choice. There is lots of scope for companies to build pages around their own product areas and services then link them back to their own websites.

These pages rank well in their own rights and provide a different source of traffic.

You have to make the pages useful and provide some good quality content. If you have news feeds or a blog feed you can easily include it on these pages too!

14. **Start a Blog**

Blogging is a great way to crate and manage a website without much in the way of technical knowledge or costs. Sites such as blogger.com, wordpress.com and typepad.com allow anyone to build and run a free blog. Write useful small posts on a given topic or even keyword based. Add a link back to your main website from each post. Make sure you promote your blog too!

You can use WordPress free on your own web server so this will allow you to run a blog as either sub directory or a sub domain

Sub Directory

http://www.mywebsite.com/blog

Sub Domain

http://blog.mywebsite.com

15. **Trade some Links**

Find some useful, relevant sites in your area and trade links. Make sure they are in the finance or insurance space. Don't trade links with sheet metal workers or florists. There really is no point!

Use a link swap directory site such as

www.linkmarket.net

to identify possible partners. Don't get too

carried away with this technique. Only find 5 - 10 useful and - most importantly - relevant links and trade.

16.   **Run a Contest**

Run a contest or competition to attract newsletter subscribers or visitors. Offer something with a perceived high value that you can get at a low cost or maybe partner up with someone. Offer to carry out a joint venture with a local electrical supplier. You promote the contest online and by issuing a press release, and put flyers up in the office window if you have client footfall. Your partner gets coverage too – and they provide the prize.

Places to submit contests to online include your own website - add a brief bit on your homepage and on your social media pages. Drive people to the site to fill in the form. Have a short easy to answer question.

17.   **Newsletters**

Offer a monthly email newsletter to your current clients and prospects. Provide them with useful articles each month on a range of topics and include a small enquiry form. Encourage people to share or pass these on to friends and family. This is a great way of staying touch and teaching your clients about all the services you offer. Try and make them seasonal and product related so that you are maximising your ability to sell. Where possible provide links back to your site for getting quotes etc.

18. **Podcasting**

There are lots of low cost and free software that allows you to record an audio file. Maybe you can put out your Newsletter as an audio file. Get a member of staff to record something each month. Publish it on your website and invite people to download it and spread the word.

Using a podcast can be seen to be a monthly little radio show. You can get clever and even record interviews with related businesses such as accountants, estate agents, or solicitors.

For a good free tool for recording audio using a PC, try downloading Audacity:

http://audacity.sourceforge.net

19. **Google My Business**

As part of Local Search, Google My Business is a great way to get your site listed locally. Sometimes for certain services when you get Google results, the first thing that appears is a map. You want to be on that map for your business.

Visit : https://www.google.co.uk/business/

Follow the instructions. It should only take a couple of minutes and you could be appearing on Google Business within a few weeks. You have the options to add images, reviews and video. Try to add as much as possible to create a fully rounded listing.

20.   **Google Analytics**

Using a free Google Analytics account, you will be able to see who visits your site, where they go and what they do. The data this thing captures for you for free is fantastic AND THERE IS NO EXCUSE NOT TO USE IT. Find out what you most popular pages are and what the leakage points are.

Without stats and analysing your site once a week or every fortnight, you could be losing lots of potential business.

Visit: www.google.com/analytics

21.   **Social Media Strategy**

Does your company have a policy on social media? Do your staff use Facebook or Twitter? Do they mention your company on their pages? This could be a good thing but it could also be a bad thing. Check the pages and see what is being said about you.

Social Media sites can drive web traffic and enhance your brand, and you should think about having a corporate profile page on

Facebook and Twitter. You should also look at business social media sites such as LinkedIn too.

Visit:
www.twitter.com
www.linkedin.com
www.facebook.com

22.   Video Marketing

With the rise of camera phones and cheap video gadgets, creating video has become simple. With popular sites such as YouTube (which generates more traffic than Google!), you could create and run a monthly video newsletter or create adhoc videos to explain key facts. Some sites even run their own video news stories and publish them online.

This is a great way to drive traffic and interest to your website.

You can either use a cheap webcam, or go a bit more up market, and use a camcorder which you can pick up these days for a couple of hundred pounds. Lighting and backdrop can set your video apart from others, so may be find somewhere in your office that you can use permanently or easily.

You can even post or host videos on Facebook or run your own live events using Facebook Live.

23. PPC – Pay Per Click

While most companies online will have heard of Google's Pay per click service, Adwords, there are other services out there that can generate a level of traffic.

Bing have their own offering of pay per click ads under BingAds

www.bingads.com

But there are other smaller sites that can generate traffic and your competition probably won't be using them. With small amounts of traffic they will be cheaper too!

Try www.7search.com, www.advertising.com, www.bidvertiser.com, www.facebook.com/ads

While some of these sites are US based, they do get UK based traffic.

24. PPC Landing Pages

Most beginners at PPC or those that manage it in house do not build dedicated landing pages for their Pay Per Click campaigns. This is a big mistake. Traffic that you are paying for is targeted so you need to make sure the place they land on your site is targeted to them too. Don't just send everyone to your homepage.

Cut their options down when they arrive. Give them one or two things to do only! Try removing phone numbers and the main site navigation. Give then a button for an enquiry form or a click to get a quote link, that's it!

Make it really easy for them to do what you want them to.

25.   Lead Buying

There has been a large number of lead companies springing up in the UK over the last few years. They could be a good source of business for you but you need to bear in mind a few things first:

Where do they source their leads?
Are you buying a unique lead or will it be sold multiple times?
How old are the leads?
How well do you convert leads generally?

26.   Affiliate Programmes

Earn money from Affiliate Programmes. Add directory pages to your website with links to household brand names. Most major household finance and insurance companies offer Affiliate deals, so you could earn commission by referring customers on non-competing products such as credit cards or bank accounts.

Visit:

www.affiliatewindow.com
www.tradedoubler.co.uk

www.uk.cj.com

for programmes.

27.   **Run your Own Affiliate Programme**

Following on from point number 26, you could setup and run your own affiliate programme. Work out what you want to attract and then work out how much you can afford to pay. Will it be a cost per click, cost per sale or cost per acquisition in the case of lead generation?

Do you want to run your own in house programme or use a network?

There are advantages and disadvantages of both, so you need to do your research. For managed network campaigns visit:

www.affili.net/uk
www.tradedoubler.co.uk

To run your own affiliate programme you will need a piece of software to run your programme. Try:

www.idevdirect.com

Read more on this here:
www.speedieconsulting.co.uk/affiliate-marketing/

28.   **Multiple Network and In-house Affiliate Programmes**

There are several companies that run in-house AND network programmes. This is a great way to get access to a large number of affiliates quickly.

You could manage the in-house programme for select volume clients where you could pay them a different level of commissions.

There are also companies that run multiple network programmes, so this could also be a way of you extending your reach.

29.   **Forum Marketing**

Taking part in relevant forums are also another good way to highlight your expertise, products and services. Unlike most other forms of marketing though, you have to be discreet about it. Overly blatant advertising is frowned upon. Become a valuable asset to the forum, answer questions and generally be helpful. After a while, add a forum signature to link to your website, blog and main products. If you want, add a phone number. This will then be included on any posts you make on the site.

Make the links, keyword links and they could have a positive SEO impact on your site too, so you could be getting a little bonus traffic!

30.   **Blog Comments**

Blog commenting used to be a great way to build inbound links to your website. These days, thanks to those that love to abuse the system, they are pretty worthless for SEO benefits. That said, a well placed and thoughtful comment to a relevant blog post could drive you direct traffic.

The easiest way to see relevant blog posts to comment upon quickly is to sign up with Google News Alerts. When you signup you get the option to receive "news alerts" or "news and blog alerts". Select "news and blog" and set to once every day. Select your keywords and then each day Google will send you, free or charge, daily posts that it has picked up and then you can visit the links and comment upon them.

I would suggest doing maybe 1 or 2 a day max.

31.   Teleseminars / Webinars

Running a teleseminar or webinar is a great way to:

- Provide your clients with a useful service
- Attract new clients
- Provide as a free gift
- Sell as a separate information product.

A teleseminar is basically using a bridge phone line with conference facilities but you want to choose one that will record the call. In this way you can upload it to your website as a giveaway.

You may even simply want to interview someone in the office to create an audio which you can use as a seminar recording.

For conference phone lines try:

www.conferenceuk.com
www.conferencegenie.co.uk

For audio recording software, try using Audacity which is free and easy to use:

http://audacity.sourceforge.net

32. Referrals

Asking for business is sometimes something we don't like doing, but it can be done quickly and easily using email. It is up to you whether you want to incentivise the referral by giving something in return or if you have enough goodwill, maybe just ask.

What ever you do make sure you stay consistent in your approach.

You can add a section to your website, try using a "tell a friend" script and just amend it to suit your purpose. There are some great free scripts out there you can use to do this.

This is the one I use with WordPress:

https://wordpress.org/plugins/wp-tell-a-friend-popup-form/

It is free and easy to operate.

Or you could try a something with a lot more powerful features such as

http://www.invitereferrals.com/

33.   Testimonials

Testimonials are a great tool to attract business. Used on your website, they can be a very powerful persuader for those prospects that are sat on the fence.

You can simply ask for testimonials at regular intervals but normally the best time is right after you have carried out business for a client. Hopefully they had a good experience and therefore would be happy to write you a testimonial.

The most powerful testimonials are specific and have the full name of the person giving the testimonial. In the modern world of the Internet, you can even add Audio or Video testimonials.

34.   Publish Documents Online

There are places online where you can publish Word Documents, Adobe PDF files and a whole range of other documents. These sites rank highly on the major search engines and are another way for you to drive traffic and attain rankings for your website.

Have a look at some of the documents you have on your computer, could these be used to promote your business?

To get some ideas look at www.scribd.com or www.slideshare.net or www.issuu.com

35. PowerPoint Presentations to create flash movies

A low cost way to create movies to be submitted to video sites is to use PowerPoint to create slideshows that can include audio and other bits. Or use screen capture software

Visit

http://www.techsmith.com/camtasia.asp

or

http://www.techsmith.com/jing.html

These could be client presentations or a range of bullet point lists. Use the produced files on promoting your business on YouTube, Facebook or Vimeo, as well as using them on your own website.

36. Run your own social networking site for Clients

You can easily create a complete social networking solution for your clients to use. In this way they can communicate with each other and it is another value added proposition. It can also be used as a way of educating them or offering them new products and services.

For a free solution look at www.ning.com

For a totally brandable solution look at the low cost option www.phpfox.com

37.   Affiliate landing pages

If you run your own affiliate programme, one thing to look at it the landing pages for your affiliates. One thing some companies forget is to make sure the landing pages work hard for your business. Make specific landing pages; do not just point people to your homepage.

Also make sure the actions are clear and easy. Don't give the visitors too many options and make sure each option you give the visitors are trackable to the affiliate. Not doing this can switch affiliates off promoting your program if you have phone numbers everywhere and they are not trackable.

38.   Joint Ventures

Are there other businesses in your area that have the same type of client you are looking for? Rather than spend lots of advertising money trying to get access to them, approach the company and set up a joint venture. This could involve creating some white labelled pages for the company in order for them to promote the venture. Normally these types of arrangements are paid on a 50/50 basis.

39.   Offer White Label Solutions

Following on from above, there could be instances where you want to build direct relationships with performing affiliates. Offering white labelled functionality could be a good motivator. They get additional content and their users feel they are staying on their site and you get the additional business.

It could also be a good way to tie in companies into a 12 month relationship.

40.   **Create Free Reports**

Free reports are great ways to promote your business, build a mailing list or to sell affiliate products. Simply create a report in Microsoft word and add links back to your site or affiliate product links and then save it as an Adobe PDF, in this way, any one can read it and share it with others.

Reports are quick and easy, and a great way to showcase your expertise and business in a low cost way.

41.   **Offer Free Courses**

Free Courses are also a great way to attract new clients and promote your business. Simply put a course could be a bunch of emails spread over the course of a few days or weeks. In fact, this note is part of a course!

To deliver this course automatically to anyone who requests it, you would need to get hold of an autoresponder service which are fairly low cost and totally automate the whole process so that once you have written and uploaded the course, it runs itself.

Courses are also good to include enquiry forms, contact details and affiliate product links so they can be earning you an income without your involvement.

Look at www.getresponse.com

42.   Build and offer a Web Toolbar

A toolbar, is a small tool that sits within a web browser for anyone who downloads it. It is brandable and always visible to a user. Benefits of a toolbar include: Driving customers back to your website, keeps your website in Front of your customers, and you can make money from promotions in your toolbar

There are lots of places where you can submit your toolbar application to drive and build links back to your site. It can be a useful tool for clients too! You just need to make it functional and worthwhile for a user to download and run it.

Visit www.mactelabs.com

43.   Desktop Marketing

Desktop Marketing solutions are an exclusive, private network communication channel with your loyal subscribers and customers which can be completely branded in your own look and feel.

Subscribers receive messages only from companies they trust. No spam, no pop-ups, and no third-party ads... just legitimate messages from a sender they want to hear from. And companies get to deliver their messages without ISPs or e-mail filters getting in the way.

While e-mail is still a powerful marketing tool, these days you need to work harder than ever to keep in touch with your list of customers and subscribers.

Here's a few reasons why:

Subscribers change their e-mail addresses, leaving you without a way to contact them.

Your legitimate messages get wrongfully trashed by overactive junk mail filters.

People's free e-mail accounts fill up quickly, causing your messages to bounce back.

For Desktop marketing consoles, there really is only one company at the moment that provides you with a software solution that works, is functional and is cost effective to purchase – PushCrew. The best part is that this technology is SO NEW that only the wealthy Fortune 500 companies have used it until now... So people using it to send promotions to their customers and subscribers now have an incredible "first-to-market" advantage over their competitors -- at least until the rest of the small-business market catches on!

One of the newer versions is www.pushcrew.com

44.   **RSS Marketing**

RSS as a content delivery method for communicating with subscribers, customers, prospects and partners that will get your content delivered and provides you with multiple new content delivery & business development opportunities. Using RSS readers, users will be able to subscribe to your feeds. No more worries about email spam filters.

RSS can also act as a promotional/visibility tool that increases your web traffic by improving your search engine rankings, generating traffic from new RSS specific sites and getting your content syndicated on other sites.

Most Blog solutions now offer RSS feeds as standard. To learn more about who to build your own RSS Feed visit:

45.   **Build a Directory**

Why not build a useful directory of associated
or complementary businesses? Let companies
add their own details. Some scripts allow
descriptions of up to 1000 words and these can
be split into separate pages.

Try www.ocportal.com or www.esyndicat.com
for a FREE version to get you started. Keep the
directory tight to your product area or location.

Don't try and mimic Yahoo! - build a quality
Niche Directory. Less, truly, is more! Invite sites
you want to appear in the directory to submit
their details. Don't just add them to your site; let
them add their own content.

46.   **Paid Advertising**

As well as PPC advertising, there still seems to
be a market place for banner advertising but
as it is not as effective as PPC, it can be very
cheap to run a large campaign across a range
of sites.

Sites such as www.valueclick.com and Google
have a huge banner display network that can
offer a range of banner ad related services.
You can also find some interesting niche sites in
your field that you can advertise on cheaply if
you spend a bit of time looking around.

Find sites that your clients use or that your ideal client would use and find out if you can advertise.

You can also use sites such as Facebook and LinkedIn to create very targeted advertising campaigns. Use the same approach for the landing pages as you would for a PPC campaign. Don't send this traffic to your homepage.

47.   Forums

One thing that gets a site interactive quicker than anything else is the addition of a forum or bulletin board. Giving visitors a platform to discuss your product, services and marketplace in general is a great way to build traffic. Some sites even use a facility to build and send out newsletters to their registered users based upon their Forums.

Try www.phpbb.com which is a very high powered piece of software and is FREE to use, or if you have a Wordpress site look at www.bbpress.org

48.   Wikipedia Listing

Submitting your company information to Wikipedia is a good way to boost the popularity of your website in the eyes of the major search engines. The challenge is that it is quite difficult to get into, as it is a humanly edited directory. You need to make sure you follow the rules before submitting. Take some time out to make sure you get it right!

Visit: www.wikipedia.org

49.   **Signature Email**

You can use your email signature file outside of just email to help drive you traffic and boost your Search Engine Rankings, so let's look at that in a bit more detail.

If you use Web Forums, Newsgroups or Classified Ads, you can use your signature file in some of these to promote your services. You will need to check the terms and conditions on the forums but if others are using an HTML footer, then you can probably do that to. So how does this help you?

In two ways really. Firstly, it allows you to place your site links on these forums pages which can build your Inbound links to your website. More Inbound links to your site from different sources the better.

Secondly, some of these forums pages rank really, really, highly in Google and the other search engines so having your link on these pages could attract you some traffic directly, which is nice!

50.   **Content updates**

Make sure you are adding content to your site on a regular basis and changing your existing site pages to reflect changes in the industry. Lots of out of date product pages will not help you.

Add articles to your site, or a unique news feed to keep your site up to date and fresh. Search engines love new original content! Give it to them!

51.   User Generated Content

There are different ways of allowing others to add their content to your site, if you run a blog site such as Wordpress you can allow comments. There are other scripts that will allow people to leave comments on certain pages.

With the advent of Blogs came the ability to leave a comment on your posts, which helped build the content on your site. Now, there are scripts around that you can add to your site pages, such as article or product review pages, and allow visitors to leave comments. This then means that your pages are changing constantly and a changing page is as good as a new page for the search engine spiders.

52.   Micro Sites

Your business might benefit from having a range of websites, each specifically targeted to a single product or service area. These "mini" or "micro" sites are a great tool to allow you to try and attain higher search engine rankings. This is because it is easier for search engine to figure out what your site is about if it is tightly themed on a single topic.

Using a tool such as Wordpress is a good way to build low cost mini sites.

Visit www.wordpress.org

Summary

We hope you find these tips useful. While not an exhaustive list of all marketing methods and techniques available online, we have selected 52 tips - so you look at one each week. So over the course of a year you could add a large number of different sources of traffic and revenue to your website.

Some will require reading but all can be implemented or tested very quickly.

Good Luck!

Bonus articles

What follows are more detailed sections on insurance marketing activities you can use to grow your business.

These have been taken from a range of articles I have written for different sites and updated them recently just for this book...

WordPress Plugins you need to be using on your Insurance website

We are seeing more and more insurance brokers using WordPress to power their websites, which is a really good thing.

However, simply using WordPress is not enough – there are a number of ways you can enhance the power of your WordPress installation to help drive traffic and sales.

There are a number of plugins we recommend site owners use to really help their sites. With nearly 50,000 plugins in the WordPress plugin directory and countless numbers outside of it, it is hard to find the best plugins for your needs.

We have been building WordPress sites for clients for nearly 10 years and now have come up with a number of go-to plugins to help a site run smoothly and to get the site working as hard as possible to drive traffic, engage with visitors and get them to take action.

It can then feed into marketing automation funnels to really drive traffic and sales.

We have split these into operational and marketing plugins – some are free but there are some paid for plugins we recommend, and they will be easily worth their investment.

Operational Plugins

Now you may not be managing your WordPress site yourself but you might want to check with your site developers to ensure you have these operational plugins in place as they can really help.

Database Optimisation

When setting up a new WordPress site, there can be a lot of amends initially to get a site live and with changes to content. WordPress is great in that is stores all your amends. But after time this can 'bloat' your site. So like a trashcan on your computer, you want to empty it out from time to time. We use a plugin to do this for us, which can free up a lot of space and speed up your site.

WP Optimise – you don't need to run it all the time, but every couple of months if you are adding regular content and making changes, it is worth rerunning it.

Caching

With site load speeds being a growing key factor in Google rankings, having pages that load quickly are a strategy for helping to get higher rankings in Google. Caching basically allows you to deliver pages much quicker.

There are a number of plugins available but we like either W3 Total Cache or WP SuperCache. One thing we always suggest is if you make changes to existing site pages or posts, to flush the cache out – otherwise sometimes your changes don't show up on the site and you can spend a while scratching your head.

Site Backups

One of the key things is to make sure you take regular site backups. With plugins you can automate this operation to run a backup and then automatically have uploaded to a secure space such as Dropbox or Google Drive. In this way, you are having a site backed up and stored offsite – weekly or monthly depending how often you are updating your site.

Backup Buddy – one of the most popular WordPress back up plugin , it is a paid for service but allows you to backup and restore sites if you need to, as well as having a great premium support service. It is also not a subscription model so you just pay for it once and you are done.

BackWPUp – is a free easy to use plugin that will allow you to set up backups and send them to Dropbox, GoogleDrive or Amazon for storage. They also have a pro version to help with restores if you need it.

Site Security

With WordPress being an open source and very popular, there are lots of people that try and exploit site weaknesses through unsecure installations; via plugin backdoors; or, trying to drop malware on your site.

These security issues are there on all sites not just WordPress ones, but the WordPress community works hard to fight them, so making sure you have the latest stable version of WordPress installed and updated plugins is one way to ensure you reduce your risks. The other is using a plugin to help your site stay secure.

Do ensure you check your WordPress dashboard regularly to see if you have recommended core or plugin updates. These could be in response to a potential security issue.

There are two products on the market we recommend. Both have free versions and paid for versions. It is your choice which option you choose from.

If you have had your site hacked you might want to look at the paid for options which can first clean your site before securing it against further issues.

WordFence – offers a free level service to protect your website from a range of potential hacks, malware and denial of service attacks. The free version is a great starting point to protect your site. The premium levels then takes this a next step further and offers live scanning of your site to give you that extra peace of mind about site security.

Sucuri – is a great tool if you have had your site hacked and need to it cleaned before having it secured. Sucuri have a range of paid, managed services to help secure your website and then protect it ongoing.

Marketing Plugins

While the main reason you used WordPress for your site was for its free, open source and easy to use content management system, the main reason we recommend it and use it for clients is its ability support your marketing efforts.

Here are the plugins we recommend you use. If you see a plugin you are not using because you are not using that marketing activity such as email newsletters or social media posting, you should look hard at these things as WordPress can do a lot of the work for you.

Lead Generation

One of the key ways to see if your website is working for you is to simply count the number of enquiries or leads it is generating for you. If you are not able to do that, it will be hard to justify any marketing investment. The easiest way to manage this is to use a form system that allows you to not only send your enquiries via email, but also store them in the WordPress backend – that way you can a backup of all your leads that can then be easily exported in the CSV or XLS so you can see where your leads are coming from.

We also recommend a system that allows it to integrate with other tools and services to really automate some of your marketing efforts.

Gravity Forms – this is our go-to form management and build plugin and have used it since day one. It allows you to create easy or complex multi page forms easily. It has extra plugins to connect forms with other services such as Mailchimp, Dropbox, Paypal, Zapier, and huge number of other tools.

ThriveLeads – this allows you to easily add in calls to actions on your site for newsletter sign ups or content reveals / locks (get extra content revealed if you signup or download an expanded version of this content via email) which is great for building your newsletter lists or driving specific enquiries. It connects to your major autoresponder services such as Mailchimp and GetResponse.

AffiliateWP – if you have considered running your own affiliate programme but feel you can't justify affiliate network costs or you don't have control over the quote and buy system which would mean you can't add tracking facilities, you could set up a lead based affiliate programme. We talk a lot more about that here, but for now let me just say AffiliateWP is the go-to tool to allow you to setup and run a lead based affiliate programme.

Email Marketing

Email marketing, while thought of as 'old school' these days by some, is still a great way to engage and stay in touch with customer and potential customers. Email newsletters can be a great way to drive leads, sales and getting people back to your site. Your website should be making every effort to get people into your email newsletter database.

The beauty is there are a number of tools that can integrate with WordPress to make it seamless and hands free. Using a tool such as Mailchimp will allow people to manage their subscriptions and remove themselves from your list, while keeping you compliant.

You can set up multiple lists so you can have a prospects list, a client list and / or a renewals list – so you can be sending different content to different groups of people.

Mailchimp – the Mailchimp plugin allows you to connect your forms on your website into your email lists in Mailchimp so any lead that comes in can be automatically added to your email newsletter list or can be added to a autoresponder sequence to follow up with a prospect on a particular enquiry.

This is a great way to automate part of your online marketing follow ups. If you don't have a Mailchimp account you can get one here. Initially you can set one up for free.

GetResponse – another email newsletter management service which has a plugin to allow API connection so that your site forms can feed your email databases.

Getresponse also has marketing automation tools built in so you can easily carry out quite complex follow ups with enquirers depending on what actions they do or don't take.

Again if you don't have a GetResponse account you can set up a free trial here.

Sendgrid – Sendgrid is one of those tools we recently came across to help emails from web forms make sure they are delivered. Sometimes forms just don't send email, and it is not a server issue or an email issue.

This can be frustrating as you know people are filling in your forms but they are simply not arriving. Sendgrid allows you to set up a free account to connect your forms system to it and you send the email via Sendgrid. In this way, it is guaranteed to be delivered. You can sign up for a free account here.

Social Media

One thing a WordPress site can really help with is supporting your social media efforts, yet this is one of the most overlooked elements. There are a number of plugins that can automatically share content when it is posted. This allows you to be consistent and making sure you are sharing your content as far and wide as possible. Here are just a few plugins you can and should utilise to help you.

SNAP – Social Media Auto Poster (SNAP) does pretty much what it says on the tin – it will autoshare your content as soon as it goes live on any number of platforms you set up. There are two versions and we always recommend to clients they go 'Pro' as it will have many more options to share across platforms and scheduled posts, and even older posts too.

Revive Old Post – As well as SNAP, Revive Old Post is a tool you can configure to allow it to reshare your older content This means you can be driving more people back to you site and helps you to reengage and get your content working harder for you. Again they have a 'Pro' version which will allow you to share across more than one platform at a time.

Mashshare – this plugin allows you to add really nice looking social share buttons and counts on your site at the top and bottom of your posts and pages if you choose. It is a great way to get people sharing your content across social media. You can set up each page to deliver the right image, link and message so when it is shared, you stand the best chance of other people clicking on your content and visiting your site.

Click to Tweet – this plugin allows you to set up short code that site visits can simply click on to tweet. This works well with quotes or data. Again, it is about sharing your site content across social media, so having a range of ways for people to do this is only a good thing. This doesn't impact on your visitors' journey and is quick and simple to do.

Content Marketing

As well as simply adding content, there will be times where you need your content to be better presented or give users options so they can better navigate it. Especially, like this article you are reading now, which is a few thousand words. You want the content to be easy to move around.

The other thing you want to do is get people deeper into your content, so adding in options for reading more relevant content and other related posts is a great way to increase the amount of time people spend on your site. This is a good thing in the eyes of Google if nothing else.

Inline Related Posts – allows you to automatically set up placements on your pages with links to relevant content. It allows up to 3 extra links to be added at the top, middle and bottom of your content and is a useful way to get people moving around your site. And it is set and forget, meaning the system will add links for you.

WP Author Box – if you have multiple authors on your website, you can add an author box to showcase the author to your readers. This plugin allows for a range of great formatted options including social media contact buttons to really boost the effectiveness of an author box. This is also useful if you allow guest authors to post.

Table of Contents – this is a great plugin if you have a large piece of content. By using different H tag headers, you can automatically add a clickable table of contents to your pages. You don't have to use it on all pages but those where you have a large amount of content on one page, it can be a useful way for users to navigate the page.

WordPress CTA – Call To Action (CTA) is the reason for every piece of content on your website, or at least it should be. These calls to actions can be calls, email sign ups, email enquiries or quote and buy online.   But these will need to stand out and WordPress CTA plugin is a valuable tool to help create calls to action that work.

YoastSEO – Last but by no means least, we recommend YoastSEO. This plugin helps you create content that it feels is more Google friendly. It uses a traffic light system to help you identify ways to improve your onsite SEO scores. It is a useful tool to help you find ways to improve your rankings.

That said, we also find it is not always worth worrying too much about green lighting pages at the expense of good copy.

YoastSEO also helps by connecting your Google Analytics and Webmaster tool accounts and can create and submit XML sitemaps for you as well. They have a free version and a Pro version – we tend to find we can get all we need from it via the free version.

Summary

There are a large number of add on plugins that can really boost your site's effectiveness and provide that return on marketing investment. Spending some time investigating these tools and deploying them on your WordPress site can really drive more traffic and engagement with your site traffic.

Facebook Chat Bots and Your Business

Are bots the compliant way to run client social media communication in the insurance industry?

One of the worries for insurance companies in using social media is not to get themselves into any trouble with the FCA. While there are FCA published guidelines on using social media, it is still seen as a grey area. One way you may be able to structure your social media client or new customer enquiry engagement on Facebook is to use bots. This article looks at what a bot is, how you can easily create one for your business, and how you can use them on Facebook.

What is a chat bot?

A chat bot is a small piece of software that is configured to interact with users who can ask simple text based questions and the bot will respond with prewritten responses that can include links, images and videos.

They can be multi-level – so if the user asks something, they get a response and then you can have the bot follow up with another question based on the previous answer so that can be presented with something else – so it can be quite a complex interaction but based on a simple flow of questions and answers. Think of it like an interactive flowchart.

Even simple bots can free up a lot of time dealing with easy questions and move potential clients further along the buying process.

How to use a chat bot?

As they can be accessed by clicking on a web link, you can easily share a link to your bot in your marketing and support materials.

These work really well on mobile devices as it is basically a Facebook Messenger service. This can be a great value-add for claims support, perhaps. Or, could work fantastically well for real time chats for travel clients looking for initial help with claims outside of office hours for example.

Other uses for a bot include:

- starting a conversation around a product or service;
- using it as a virtual assistant to deal with basic user enquiries;
- handling frequently asked questions;
- educating customers on a new product or service and then handling any enquiries.

Right now the only limit to your bot is your imagination. The beauty from a compliance point of view is as each action and response is pre scripted, so these interactions can be compliance checked and approved before putting your bot live.

There are a growing number of services you can use to easily build a bot. There are a number of free solutions. We have played with two of them and they are listed below. Both work in similar ways and their output via Facebook is similar.

The key to success is the time and effort you put into structuring the bot sequences. Also it should be said, you don't have to have one bot doing it all.

You could have a number of bots doing specific tasks for you.

ManyChat - https://manychat.com/
ChatFuel – https://www.chatfuel.com/

Promoting a chatbot and building an audience

Once you have built your chatbot, you should look to promote it in the same way you do with other marketing tools or content.

Clearly Facebook advertising is a key way as it is a Facebook messenger based bot service we are highlighting, but contact your customers via email to say you now have a Bot available to help them manage their claims enquiries with a link to it can be a great way to build up an audience. Write about it on your blog. You can even send them a SMS message with a link to it if you need to.

Also add a link to it on your website at the relevant key points. Share it on your social media channels and you can even submit it to bot directories so those people looking for a bot can find you. Here is a bot directory you can submit your bot to in order to get you started.

The added benefits of both Manychat and Chatfuel is they will show you who is interacting with your bots so you can see how effective they are at carrying out their tasks for you.

Summary

Facebook is really the tip of the iceberg with bots. There are facilities and technology so you can build a standalone bot, but for now there is a huge amount of scope for bots interacting with Facebook users. It could be a great way to attract new business or help maintain customer service with existing ones.

Lead Buying or Lead Generating

If your business needs leads to survive, then you have two main ways of driving them. You can buy leads in from lead generation companies, or you can generate leads yourself. From property, to finance, to insurance, leads can be the way you need to engage with prospects as you might not be able to offer quote and buy on line facilities.

But leads, either bought or generated, can be a real problem:

- if you don't know where the leads are coming from;
- as you don't know how they are being generated;
- as you don't know who else could be getting them;
- if you don't have the real system in place to manage them or convert them.

Buying or Generating – an overview of the advantages and disadvantages

Buying

Advantages

- Can be quick to setup
- Can get leads the same day
- Can fix costs

Disadvantages

- Can be poor quality
- Can be hard to convert

- You might not own the data – the lead generation company might solicit the data next year or you might not be able to cross sell products

Generating

Advantages

- Generating unique leads
- Not sharing them with other brokers
- Building your business not others

Disadvantages

- Can take a while to start seeing leads
- Need to develop more skills in the business
- No fixed costs initially

Buying Leads

There are a large number of lead generation companies in the UK that will sell you leads for a huge number of different products.   There are some things you need to understand, however, before you buy leads. Now I'm not suggesting lead companies are bad and evil, but I would say before you enter into buying leads you need to understand exactly what you are buying.

Questions to ask before buying a lead

How are the leads being generated?

This is a key question and if a company cannot tell you how and show you an example site with how these leads are being generated – run!

Who else is getting this lead?

Are you the only company getting the lead? You could be shocked to know that lead companies can and have a policy to sell the same lead up to 3 or 4 times, so in essence you are in competition with 3 or 4 other companies to get to the lead. This doesn't mean it is a no go, but you need to understand you will need to get on to these leads as soon as they come into your inbox.

Be honest with yourself – will you be able to hit them hard and fast? If not, think twice.

Can I filter leads?

You maybe have a niche of lead types or you many need a particular geographic area. Can you filter the leads so you only get what you can service? Most companies will have some kind of filtering process available. Make sure you ask – you don't have to take everything they throw at you.

How are the leads delivered?

Understand how the lead will arrive and test to make sure they do. I have seen horror stories of companies not realizing leads were being sent so didn't do anything with them until they got big invoice at the end of the month from the lead generation company. Test, test and test again.

Companies that sell leads

Listed below are lead generation companies we have worked with on behalf of clients. Please do you own due diligence as things change and there are plenty of stories – good or bad on – lead generation companies. Hence this article. Check forums, Google them and if there is something you don't like, move onto the next one.

Quotezone – http://www.seopa.com/join/buy-sell-leads.html

Landlord Today – https://www.landlordtoday.co.uk/advertise-with-us

Mortgage Angels – http://www.mortgageangels.co.uk/advisers

VouchedFor – https://www.vouchedfor.co.uk

Efinity Leads – http://www.e-finityleads.co.uk

SO Leads – http://www.simplyonlineleads.com

Call Credit – http://www.callcredit.co.uk/products-and-services/consumer-marketing-data/online-lead-generation

Generating your own leads

Make sure your site is ready for leads.

The first thing is to take along hard look at your current website. Is it fit for purpose – does it already generate leads? If it doesn't, then it might need changing or amending to be more lead focused.

The biggest issue we see is that websites tend to start out as nothing more than brochureware, so it is online pamphlet of your business, when you need to it to do much more and capture leads and enquiries and then follow up with them.

Your website can do a lot of the heavy lifting for you if it is set up correctly. We always recommend that clients looking to get into lead generation use the same basic formula to build their lead gen website

WordPress + Gravity Forms = Lead Gen Machine

This can be any type of lead generation site. WordPress is a fantastic tool to build and manage a website and using Gravity Forms will allow you to create forms and then allow you to manage them as you need to.

Once you have your new website, you can look at the various options for driving traffic and, ultimately, leads.

Range of traffic options

Here are a few of the main options you can use to drive traffic to a website.

- SEO
- PPC Marketing
- Social Media
- Affiliate Programmes
- Email Marketing
- Content Discovery
- Referral Programmes

I would suggest a few things

- Test one or two options before adding any more

- Don't simply rely on one source of traffic – it will not last forever so divest yourself of more than one source
- Make sure you have tracking in place to show you what is working and what isn't – this can simply be Google Analytics

Summary

Lead generation can be a great addition to your marketing arsenal and a viable way to drive your business forward. I hope this article gives you some food for thought before engaging with any lead buying company so you can go in 100% knowing what you are paying for. If you want some help building your own lead generation efforts please feel free to get in touch.

Email marketing for insurance companies

Isn't it frustrating that you have launched a new product or written a new blog post and it gets no traffic?

In this article, let's take a look at how your existing customer base and site traffic can be used to generate product interest and even traffic to your website consistently.

Most sites will drive some traffic and get some enquiries but will do very little beyond trying to get site visitors to fill in an enquiry form or run a quote. If this is the main driver of the site, then for every 100 people that visit the site possibly 95 of them will leave without enquiring or carrying out a quote. So this means your site is converting at 5% – even at 20% conversion 80 out of every 100 visitors don't do anything but leave. Quite depressing really...

If you are buying in this traffic then this does get costly...

With a few tweaks to your pages and processes, you can use this traffic to start building an email list, which you can then use to email to each week or month with targeted offers and also links to your useful blog content.

Add email or newsletter signups to your pages, which could be something simple as asking for an email address. In return you can provide something in exchange – maybe a 5% off discount code or a free downloadable checklist or guide relevant to your target audience.

In this way you are giving away something of value in return for an email address.

You do need to sell the benefits of subscribing to your list.

What do you need to get this going?

You will need some kind of email service provider (ESP) to allow you to build email capture forms, manage subscribers and allow you to send messages. There are a number of services out there. We personally use GetResponse to manage our email signups.

You also need some kind of offer or giveaway to entice your site traffic to signup to your list. This could be:

- PDF Guide
- PDF Checklist
- Discount code
- Money off voucher

In fact, you are only limited by your imagination. You could also have multiple offers depending on the type of traffic and product areas they are interested in. The offer for a business owner could be different from a caravan owner.

And by using an ESP you can segment that data, or have multiple lists you can send different content and offers to.

While this sounds like a lot of hard work, I am not going to lie, it is upfront – but once in place it is a case of building the lists and letting the system follow up.

This is done by simply driving the traffic as you have been doing.

Here are some ideas of what others in the space are doing

We would have loved to have shown UK insurance specific landing pages but there are very few doing it so here are some finance related ones..

- Love him or hate him, Martin Lewis has built a very, very successful business based in part on his newsletter. http://www.moneysavingexpert.com/

- Look at the MoneyAdviceService Email Newsletter signup – shame it is being withdrawn. This sits underneath all of the articles on the site. https://www.moneyadviceservice.org.uk/en

- Savvywoman is a personal finance site aimed at women and again there is a clear signup box on every page of the site. https://www.savvywoman.co.uk/

Taking this to the next level

Once you have these systems in place you can even have your email enquiry forms feed into your ESP as well, so each enquiry you generate will also add these enquirers to your email database.

Best practices

Use an opt-in process, so once they have signed up, the ESP can send them an email to get them to opt into receiving your information. Make sure you do this with ALL of your signups, either via an enquiry form or via the signup boxes dotted around the site.

This keeps you on the right side of the law. It is also wise to ensure users have an opt-out or unsubscribe link within any email your ESP sends out, so your newsletters and marketing messages.   Again this is best practice – it gives subscribers the ability to unsubscribe – but as you are providing huge value to them, why would they want to leave your list?

One thing we are recommending all insurance companies do is ensure their emails work on mobile devices. More and more people are accessing their email on their smartphone so do make sure your emails are correctly coded to work on both desktop computers and mobile devices. This will really improve engagement and open rates.

Email marketing

Once you are have started to collect this information you need to start emailing it consistently – don't wait until you have 1,000 email addresses, that could take 3 or 4 months to build as when you finally send out the email, people will unsubscribe as they won't remember you.

Make sure you have at least one email ready to go.   For those insurance companies starting email marketing for the first time we suggest having a monthly newsletter. In this way, you can split it into maybe 1 main offer and then 3 or 4 links to content on your site or your blog. Or you can even link to other useful and related content. In this way, you are providing real value to your users but without the need to write everything yourself.

As you can hopefully see, once you have a fair sized email list, each month you can send out links to your new content and get people back to your website.

You can also use that list to launch new products and services. You can even use the database to soft launch a product, so you can email out your list with an offer before you integrate it or invest in it fully on your website. Consider it user testing and product research all rolled into one.

Summary

Building an email database of potential clients or those interested in your products and services is a great way to increase revenues but also a great way to get your new content read and shared.

If you are driving a lot of traffic to your website and not building a email database or databases then you need to do this as a matter of urgency.

Affiliate Marketing – How to earn extra revenues by adding or promoting secondary products

Affiliate marketing can be used by businesses to increase the reach of their own products by running their own affiliate marketing programme. However, companies should also look at the other side of affiliate programmes, namely promoting other companies' products in order to add an additional revenue stream to your website.

Now while I would not suggest plastering other companies banners and marketing materials on the front end of your website, there are a number of ways you can add affiliate commissions while not detracting from your core business.

Email Newsletters

If you have an email newsletter which you send out each month, there could be an opportunity to include links to other complimentary products that might be of use to your email database. If you also confirm a purchase or lead via email you could also add some links in here as well.

Thank you pages / Offerwalls

Once a user has bought from you or made an enquiry, you can redirect them to a "thank you for your business" page. On this page you could have links to other related but not competing products. In the mobile apps space, these are called Offerwalls that have a number of adverts offering products. You can deploy this technique on your website after your main activity has occurred – such as a sale or lead enquiry.

Additional product pages

You could also consider adding additional website pages, so if your website attracts a lot of traffic or ranks very well, you could create additional product pages offering affiliate products. This could also be a great way to test out a product you could be thinking about broking directly to your audience. You can test how profitable a product could be before launching it yourself.

You could take it a step further and develop standalone websites simply promoting those products.

Blog Posts

If you a have a blog, you could write blog posts about these affiliate products and link to them. In this way it is slightly away from your main business activity but still being offered to your visitors.

Social Media

As well as blogs, you can use social media to highlight and promote affiliate offerings directly. You can create social media posts and updates that link to the blog posts or content you have written for the affiliate offers. Or you could drive traffic straight to the affiliate offers themselves. It really comes down to how aggressive you want to be in promoting other products.

Finding affiliate offers to promote

There are a large number of places to find affiliate offers. I would suggest joining an affiliate network which will have a large number of offers you could be promoting and earning commissions from.

Initially, I would recommend joining one network and promoting two or three offers to get an understanding of how well it could work. There are 4 or 5 affiliate networks in the UK that would be a good starting point:

- www.affiliatewindow.com

- www.affili.net

- www.tradedoubler.co.uk

- www.affiliatefuture.co.uk

- uk.cj.com

You could still focus on promoting various niche insurance offers that you don't want to offer yourself, but could still recommend to your audience. Here are some ideas:

AffiliateWindow
ALA Gap Insurance
Pedalsure Cycle Insurance
RAC Breakdown Insurance
WarrantyWise Car Warranty Insurance

Affili.net
Bettersafe Excess Insurance
Debenhams Wedding Insurance

Tradedoubler
Columbus Travel Insurance

Insure Learner Driver Insurance

Affiliatefuture
British Insurance Protection Insurance
Lexham insurance Moped and Scooter Insurance
SwitchedOn Gadget Insurance

CJ
Argos Pet Insurance

I hope this gives you some food for thought. Good luck. If you need help developing a strategy, please feel free to drop us a line.

Social media marketing for insurance companies

Insurance companies have a wide range of options when it comes to marketing their products and services. Whether you are a broker or you sell your own products, you can benefit from a range of marketing techniques.

Online marketing is proving increasingly popular, and especially social media. You may be wondering how exactly you can take advantage of social media marketing for your insurance business, so here are a number of ways to start seeing results.

High-value content gets results

Most online marketing revolves around content in some way or another, and social media is no different.

If you constantly create high-quality content that answers the questions your audience has, and provides the information they are seeking, you're going to be off to a good start.

You don't have to only focus on creating content. You can also curate it.

Spend time seeking out valuable content from other creators, and share this with your followers. They will appreciate it, and it won't take as long as creating your own. Don't rely on curation alone, but do make use of it.

Reach out to your targets with ads

Social media marketing has many benefits for businesses, and one of these is the ability to reach out to targets with ads.

Paid advertising is big on social networks, and it can be very useful when it comes to social media marketing for insurance companies.

Facebook, Twitter and LinkedIn all have their own marketing platforms. They all differ slightly, but they all provide you with the same basic ability to reach out to specific targets based on a wide range of demographics.

You could target people who have recently visited your website, in a technique known as retargeting. Or you could simply create compelling ads for people who you are trying to reach out to. You could even use ads to encourage more signups to your email list

Experiment with them and see what you can do. It can't hurt to try, and the rewards can be huge.

Get serious with social media management tools

One of the big problems with social media is that there are many networks and you simply don't have time in the day to send out updates, respond to comments, launch competitions, answer questions, etc.

That's where social media management tools come in.

Sendible is one of the biggest of these, and Hootsuite is another. These provide you with a huge range of tools, allowing you to schedule posts in advance and get access to details analytics.

Importantly, they also enable you to quickly find out about comments made about your brand. This allows you to respond to the comments quickly, and this is good practice for both positive and negative comments.

Maintain an active presence

These are all good techniques for getting more out of social media marketing. Perhaps the most important thing of all, however, is to stay active.

Don't dip your toe into social media from time to time, then get cold feet and disappear for weeks or months at a time. This is a daily activity.

But if you are willing to spend the time and effort on it, you may find that social marketing can really pay off.

Building your own lead generation affiliate programme using WordPress

If you are using WordPress to power your website did you know you can use two plugins to effectively manage your own lead generation affiliate programme?

For most brokers it is difficult to work with network affiliate programmes due to the tracking code that is needed to be installed to track online quote and buy sales (normally run via a third party platform – OpenGi or Acturis for example), but with lead enquiries this difficulty has been removed.

By combining Gravity Forms and AffiliateWP you can easily create landing pages, forms and tracking to allow anyone to send you leads and pay them on a per valid lead basis.

Tools you will need:

- A WordPress powered site (if you don't have one and are interested, please contact us and we can share with you some of the available options / costs)
- Gravity Forms – the form builder we recommend and use on all our client sites
- AffiliateWP – the affiliate tracking solution we recommend WordPress

We only work with WordPress sites so all of this is written around the WordPress content management system (CMS). There could be other options for other CMS but this is purely written for WordPress users.

Forms

The first thing to do is use Gravity Forms to build out your lead enquiry forms. We use Gravity Forms as it allows you to store records in the backend of WordPress, send autoresponders back to the user, email the lead you in real-time, and much, much more.

Set up a different landing page and form per product enquiry. In this way, you can build specific question sets per product – this will generate you a much more valuable lead. It will also help generate a valid lead as simple name and email leads can be hard to validate. http://www.speedieconsulting.co.uk/the-4cs-of-affiliate-marketing/
As a guide and from our experience, the more info you ask, the more you should pay for the lead but they better quality it will be. It is a fine line between quality and quantity. We always suggest quality!

Tracking

Once your forms are set up and you have dedicated thank you pages – i.e. the pages users land on once they have completed a form – we will be able to add the AffiliateWP tracking to ensure that leads coming from registered affiliates will show up correctly.

Setup your commission structure

One of the key things is to work out how much you are willing to pay for a valid lead. If you are doing other forms of online marketing you will get an idea of how much it costs you to generate a lead or you will see other lead generation businesses and how much they are charging.

The key is to stick to a commission structure. So take some time to figure out what you can afford to pay. Remember, having different forms means you can pay different amounts depending on the product. Affiliates hate having commissions being reduced after a few weeks because you got your sums wrong.

Technical help

Both Gravity Forms and AffiliateWP have great support, which is why we recommend them – or if you want the hands free approach why not get in touch and we can give you a quote to build it for you?

Now it is built and live. What is next?
You will now need to promote your programme and there are a wide range of options you can use to get the message out there. Here are some of our favourites: http://www.speedieconsulting.co.uk/attract-new-affiliates-and-then-get-them-to-put-up-your-links/
PR activity

You might want to send out a press release to say your programme is live. You can use services such as MyNewsDesk, 247 Press Release or PR Newswire.

Reach out to your contacts

Once your programme is live, share an update with your contacts, post it on your social media channels, add a site blog post, share on LinkedIn or Twitter.

Affiliate page

Add an affiliate page to your website with details on your commission structure and how to apply to the programme. I would suggest not auto approving every one and to take your time selecting affiliates. To get some ideas of what to include on your affiliate page – here are some various insurance sample pages:

http://www.comparethemarket.com/affiliates/
http://www.morethan.com/affiliates
http://www.staysure.co.uk/affiliates

Recruiting affiliates

You can also reach out to potential affiliates directly. Use Google to search your major product areas and see if there are affiliates in the rankings showing up. Then reach out to them to share your programme and invite them to join. Don't just use Google though, also use Bing and Yahoo – you will find slightly different results.

Keep on top of your programme and build it over time. You will find that you could have teething issues with quality leads but keeping on top of it and removing affiliates that generate poor quality is the best way to ensure your programme becomes an asset to your business.

The 7 pages your website needs to convert visitors to sales

Every website needs certain pages in order to convert visitors. It is no point only focusing on getting visitors to your site, and the main challenge is getting them to convert once you get them there.
Your insurance business may well depend on online conversions – so which pages do you need to have on your site?

1. Home page

The home page is often the first page that visitors will see when they land on your site. This is your chance to make a good first impression, so make it count.

The design should be attractive, and the navigation should be clear. It should lead to the other main pages like services, products, contact page, etc, so that visitors can easily find their way to where they want to go. You can also make use of high-quality images to create an impact.

2. Landing pages

Landing pages are pages that have been deliberately set up to get a conversion from each visitor, and they are often used as part of a marketing campaign.

The aim could be to collect email addresses, to send visitors to a product page to make a sale, or anything else.

They should have no navigation and just a single call to action, and you should make sure the page includes benefits, testimonials, and more to get the conversions. Here is a good guide to the elements you should include on the page.

3. About page

The about page is your chance to tell visitors about you and your business. Try not to focus on what you do, but rather why you do it. Don't provide a long, boring history, and make it personal. It is a good idea to use photos of you and your employees because this will help to build trust.

4. Product pages

http://www.speedieconsulting.co.uk/writing-blog-content/
The pages for individual products are important for making conversions. These pages should highlight the benefits of your products or services, and each page should provide all of the details in an easy-to-read format.

You could also include images and videos to describe the product, and you will want to make it clear what you want visitors to do, whether that is to contact you, get a quote or anything else.

5. Testimonials & case studies

Social proof is essential for making conversions, so make sure you include testimonials and case studies on your site.

People will want to know they can trust you, and case studies and testimonials will help with this. You could even add a page on reviews from previous customers.

6. Contact page

People want to know that they can contact you, so make it easy for them. Include as many options as possible, including:

- phone number;
- email address;
- contact form;
- social media accounts;
- instant chat.

Link to the contact page from every other page and don't make visitors search for it.

7. Blog

Publish different types of content on your blog, including a mix of educational content and sales content, like the type we can help you with at Speedie Consultants. Include text, videos, infographics, statistics, interviews and more to attract more people to your site and to encourage them to spend more time engaging with your brand.

Make more conversions on your site

These are seven crucial pages that most insurance websites need in order to make conversions. Have you got all of these pages? If you have, are they all doing what they should be? Go over your site and look at ways that you can make improvements to each of these pages, and give your conversions a boost.

15 ways to build your email subscribers list

Email marketing can be profitable for any business, no matter what kind of product or service you are promoting. It is significantly cheaper than other advertising methods and it helps build credibility with your subscribers. As a result, you can generate more sales and profits.

The foundation for successful email marketing is a targeted, responsive and permission-based email list. If you have a list of subscribers that trust you and consider you an expert, you've completed the first step and are on your way!

Below you will several list-building ideas that will help you make the most of your email marketing efforts:

1. Provide useful, relevant and unique content. Your visitors will not give you their email addresses just because they can subscribe to your newsletter free of charge. You have to provide unique and valuable information that will be useful to your subscribers.

2. Add a subscription form to every page of your website. Make sure it stands out so it is easy to find. If appropriate, you can also include it in more than one place. For instance, your opt-in form might always appear in the top-left corner of your site, while you also include an opt-in at the bottom of some of your popular articles.

3. Make it easy for your reader to sign up. The more information you request, the fewer people will opt-

in. In most cases, a name and an email address should suffice. If it's not necessary, don't include it here. (Note: If you don't have a Privacy Policy, put the words "privacy policy generator" into a search engine and you should be able to find a suitable form for your readers to review.

4. Publish a Privacy Policy. Let your readers know that they can be confident you will not share their information with others. The easiest way to do this is to set up a Privacy Policy web page and provide the link to it below your opt-in form.

5. Show your first issue or other sample to your visitors. This lets potential subscribers review your newsletter before they sign up to determine if it is something they'd be interested in.

6. Archive past newsletter issues. A "library" of past newsletters is both appealing and useful to visitors and builds your credibility as an authority. In addition, if your articles are written with good SEO techniques in mind, they can send additional traffic to your web site through good search engine positioning.

7. Contact other newsletter publishers. Introduce yourself and explore ways you may be able to help each other. Perhaps you can introduce other publisher's newsletters or print articles they have written to your list, with a link to sign up. When you contact them, be sure to tell them why you think THEIR readers would like what you have to offer and why YOUR readers would benefit from their newsletters. This is a win-win scenario; both of you will build your lists faster.

8. Give away bonuses subscribers can use. Create an opt-in bonus for joining your subscriber list. You can write an ebook or PDF report, or even hire a programmer to create downloadable or web-based software. But don't limit yourself to only a gift for new opt-ins. Remind your readers that the next bonus is coming soon. People hate to miss out on things. If you systematically pass on "goodies" throughout the year, your subscribers are unlikely to leave.

9. Ask your subscribers to pass it on. Word of mouth is a powerful viral technique that works great with email marketing. If your subscribers find the content you share with them to be informative, they will pass your newsletter on to their friends. This can be a good source of new subscribers.

10. Let others reprint your newsletter as long as the content is not modified. Many webmasters and newsletter publishers are actively looking for high-quality content and, if they reprint your newsletter, you will get new subscribers, traffic and links pointing to your site.

11. Include a "Sign Up" button in the newsletter. If you are using plain text instead of HTML, provide a text link to your subscription page. You may feel that this is not required because the subscriber is already on your list, but remember that readers will forward your newsletters to others, or reprint it online. You want to make it easy for them to subscribe.

12. Add a squeeze page. A squeeze page has one goal ? to get an opt-in and build your list. Think of it like a mini-sales letter for your subscription or opt-in

bonus. It features a powerful headline and a couple of very important benefits that should make subscribers salivate to sign up to your list. Once created, use a service such as WordTracker to find hundreds of targeted keywords, and advertise there using pay-per-click advertising from Google, MSN and Yahoo.

13. Include testimonials on your squeeze page. This is crucial. Put 1 or 2 strong testimonials from satisfied subscribers on your squeeze page. This can be in any format, but you may find that multimedia (audio or video social proof) is more "believable". To increase that believability, include full names, locations and/or urls; don't use "Bob K, FL" as a testimonial name.

14. Blog religiously. Blogging is a great way to communicate with your potential customers, and it creates a nice synergy with your email marketing. Be sure to include your newsletter sign-up form on each page of your blog. You can start a free blog at Blogger or WordPress.

15. Post on other blogs. Post great comments and information on similar blogs with a link to your squeeze or opt-in page. Also comment on others' blogs through trackbacks. In most cases, your comments will be posted on their blogs with a link back to your site. This is an easy way to generate new traffic and subscribers.

We have been using GetResponse Email Marketing for the last 10 years and NEVER had an issue with their online service. Why not visit them now and get a free trial of their service.

Using Google Adwords to help you at renewal time

During renewal time, if you are simply sending out letters to your clients with a renewal quote, and hoping to get a reply, you might be missing a few opportunities to remind them you provided their insurance 12 months ago.

We are not advocating you stopping sending renewal letters or emails, but if your renewal rate is under 50%, here are a couple of ideas you can use to help get your customers back to you using pay per click (PPC) marketing.

Retargeting

Retargeting converts site visitors into buyers. Generally 2% of visitors convert on the first visit to a website. Retargeting brings back the other 98%. And because you're targeting people who have already shown an interest in what you have to offer by visiting your site, retargeting ad campaigns are highly effective and reengaging.

Every site – whether you use retargeting or not – should have Google retargeting tags in place as it will allow you to build up a custom audience of site visitors. You can then segment this list into visitors, quoters and buyers. In this way, you can engage with them via Adwords to try and get the visitors and quoters back to the site. And if this data has been collected for a while, you will have over 12 months worth of data that will keep growing.

You can use retargeting to put your company brand in front of these people when they are using the web.

Retargeting is also not just limited to Google. Facebook has the same facility so you can cross promote. Site visitors on Google can be delivered ads on Facebook and vice versa.

This can be a great way to improve your renewal conversion rates and reach those hard to get to customers

Customer Match

Another tool in Google Adwords is the ability to upload your client email database. Any clients that use Gmail services can be targeted via GSP (Gmail Sponsored promotions) – another great way to get into your clients' inboxes at renewal time.

Gmail Sponsored Promotions

Finally, GSP can allow you to send email ads to Gmail users who could be due for renewal (and not just your renewal) – you can target potential new clients that might have received email renewal notices from their existing insurance providers.

Mobile friendly

With more and more people accessing websites online via a smartphone or mobile device, making sure your marketing messages are accessible via a mobile device is key. So emails and creative need to be actionable and responsive on a smartphone.

Hopefully this will give you some ideas so you can divert some of your current PPC spend into targeting renewals. If you want us to help you drive a higher conversion rate from your renewals or set up any of the Google products above, please complete the short form here.

Online Local Business Services for Insurance Brokers

Google allows you to list your business directly in their small business directory for free.

https://www.google.co.uk/business/

This means that if a user searches for a local business in Google, you will tend to see a map appear first with up to 10 businesses on it. Having listings in the business centre means your business could appear on the local search map. You can also see that if a searcher looks for you by name, you will get a large listing on the right hand side with much more details about your business.

With more and more users accessing the web via their mobile device or smartphone looking for businesses "near me", making sure you have a listing on the Google business platform can be a great way to drive traffic and enquiries.

Here is an example using "Insurance Thanet"

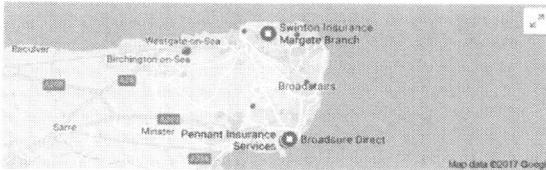

Google — Insurance Thanet

All   News   Maps   Images   Shopping   More   Settings   Tools

About 331,000 results (0.46 seconds)

MoneySuperMarket Car Insurance - Compare Cheap Quotes Here
[Ad] www.moneysupermarket.com/Cheap/Car-Insurance ▼
Compare 145+ Car Insurance Quotes and You Could Save up to £275 With Us!
Price Cuts · Compare leading providers · Free comparison service · FCA Regulated · Tailored Quotes

Rating ▼   Hours ▼

Easter Monday might affect these hours

Broadsure Direct
3.7 ★★★★ (3) · Car and Motor Insurance Agency
4.7 mi · 4th Floor, Arglye Centre · 0800 292 2235
Open until 17:30
WEBSITE   DIRECTIONS

Pennant Insurance Services
1 review · Car and Motor Insurance Agency
4.7 mi · 70 Queen St · 01843 586239
Open until 17:00
WEBSITE   DIRECTIONS

Swinton Insurance Margate Branch
1.0 ★ ★ ★ ★ ★ (2) · Insurance Agency
2.9 mi · 239 Northdown Rd · 01843 297744
Open until 17:30
WEBSITE   DIRECTIONS

☰ More places

Pennant Insurance Services: Insurance Broker Thanet
www.pennantinsurance.co.uk/ ▼
Domestic and commercial insurance services from Ramsgate in Kent

Bridges Insurance Brokers – Kent
www.bridges-insurance.co.uk/ ▼
A different approach to insurance for businesses and individuals: good value, straight-talking and
consistent care.

As you will see the first set of results returned use a map and have listings next to them. This is the integration of Google business into their search results.

You will also note that all of the paid advertising around this local search term is being bought by insurance aggregator websites so they see the power of local search but they can't take real advantage of it other than by paying for advertising. If an aggregator is paying for this traffic then it is obviously worthwhile. The bottom line is you need to make sure your site appears in local listings.

You can also do a similar thing by adding your business to both Bing and Yahoo.

You can find out more details on how to do this by using the links here:
Bing – https://www.bingplaces.com/
Yahoo (is managed by Infoserve) –
 https://www.infoserve.com/local-listings/yahoo-local/
Other places to list your site to help you appear under local terms:
Hotfrog – http://www.hotfrog.co.uk/
LocalSearch24 – http://www.localsearch24.co.uk/
Thomson Local – http://www.thomsonlocal.com/
Scoot (Scoot Network gives you a directory access to The Sun, The Independent, The Mirror, amongst others) –
 http://www.scoot.co.uk/
Touchlocal – http://www.touchlocal.com/

We hope this gives you some food for thought. Most if not all of these options have free and paid versions. It is worth at the very least completing the free options as it can drive some traffic and enquiries.

Local broker for local people

One of the strange things about the Internet is that while it gives you access to literally anything, anywhere on the Globe, it can also be a great way to find stuff that is very local to you. In this respect, this can be a great way for brokers looking for local business to get more traffic from people looking for your business.

There are a number of ways to do this. Here are a few ideas to get you started.

Local Directory Services
If you are struggling to get traffic from local listings in Google, Bing and Yahoo!, then you really need to start submitting your site to a range of local based directories. Services such as the Google My Business are a great, easy way to start getting traffic from some of the local search phrases relevant to your business. These sites tend to feature highly in local searches within Google especially so take out some time and sign up with some of the directories listed below.

Here is a small list of some of the best local based services your site needs to be featured on, in order to maximise your chances of getting traffic and business from local search.

We have broken these down into US and UK as there will be no benefit – or in some cases no way – for UK sites to submit to some of the US sites without a US postal address.

UK Local Directories

Bing – https://ssl.bing.com/listings/BusinessSearch.aspx
City Local – http://www.citiylocal.co.uk
Free Index – http://www.freeindex.co.uk
Google My Business –
 https://www.google.com/intl/en/business/
HotfrogUK –
 http://www.hotfroguk.co.uk/AddYourBusiness.aspx
My Local Services – http://www.mylocalservices.co.uk
The Best of – http://www.thebestof.co.uk
Touch Local – http://www.touchlocal.com
Applegate – https://www.applegate.co.uk
Scoot – https://www.scoot.co.uk

US Local Directories
CitySearch.com – http://www.citysearch.com
Google Maps – http://maps.google.com
InsiderPages.com – http://www.insiderpages.com
Local.com – http://www.local.com
SuperPages.com – http://www.superpages.com
Yahoo! Local – http://local.yahoo.com
Yelp – http://www.yelp.com

Onsite Contact Details
Make sure that the contact and address details for your business are the same everywhere. So if you are applying to those directories above, use the exact same address as on your website. It would be advisable to have the address on each page of your site. You can get around this by simply adding it to your footer. While this it may not look important, it really is.

The main search engines use verifiable addresses as a way to prove a business is genuine and having something the same on 10 or 15 different sites adds authority to your listing.

Get Reviews

One way to get a boost in local rankings, especially in Google, is to have local reviews of your business. But these don't simply happen – you need to ask for them. While there are services such as Feefo and Trustpilot, for smaller local brokers you can use Google itself and ask for reviews on your Google My Business page that you set up beforehand. This is an added bonus for setting up your Google My Business Profile.
https://www.google.com/intl/en/business/

Local Blog Content
Write about the local area. May be people are looking to move to the area so why not write a guide to the area, the schools etc... Why not write some content around local landmarks or local events? There is a huge amount you can do here that others won't be, and it can drive you local business
http://www.speedieconsulting.co.uk/come-and-join-the-community/

Local Networking Groups
Make sure your website and details are listed on any local networking group websites. Take it to the next levels and add links to all your group members to your site (may be set up a mini local directory) and ask them to link to you.

Facebook Advertising
Facebook allows you to advertise to people in a postcode area or radius of a town or city. In this way, you can promote your business to people in the area. This can be a fantastic way to grow your business cheaper than using advertising services such as Google Pay Per Click

Summary

There are a number of things you can do to boost your local presence online in order to drive more traffic, calls and footfall to your business. Take some time out and implement some of these ideas to boost your business.

About the Author

Jason has spent the last 18 years working with Finance and Insurance companies using the Internet. He has also worked in that time or consulted with all of the major Insurance and Finance aggregators including MoneySupermarket, Confused, MoneyExtra, Moneynet and others...

Now totally focussed on providing web based content and marketing solutions to Finance and Insurance companies. From the large online players to the smaller individual insurance broker , mortgage broker or IFA.

Our biggest services are web content, link building and lead generation for clients.

We have a range of products from blog content, email newsletters, web content and article marketing plans.

He is helping these companies with their SEO, affiliate marketing and link building campaigns.

Connect with Us

Website
http://www.speedieconsulting.co.uk

LinkedIn
https://uk.linkedin.com/in/insuranceinternetmarketing/

LinkedIn Group
https://www.linkedin.com/groups?home=&gid=3674792

Facebook Group
http://www.facebook.com/insurance.marketing

37253035R00053

Printed in Great Britain
by Amazon